Welcome to our HappyStoryGarden!

Copyright © 2024 by Viktoriia Harwood

All rights reserved.

No part of this book may be reproduced in any form or by any electronic or mechanical means, including information storage and retrieval systems, without written permission from the author, except for the use of brief quotations in a book review.

2024

Victoria Harwood

Book 2

Blame the Monster

Victoria Harwood

Monsters in this book:

1. Reflection Monster
2. Scribble-scrobble Monster
3. Monster of Whimsicality
4. Falling Cups Monster
5. Monster of Corners
6. Attic Monster
7. Monster of envy.
8. Werewolf Monster
9. Sleeve Monster
10. "Dunno" Monster
11. Puddle Monster
12. Rumble Monster

13. Shoelaces Monster
14. Flower Monster
15. Gluttony Monster
16. Begging Monster
17. Brawl Monster.
18. Monster of Boredom.
19. Resentment Monster
20. Refusal Monster.
21. Ajar doors Monster.

I'm really glad you liked the first book about monsters and you are keen to meet more!

From the first book, you have already learned much about these kind of monsters - amazing creatures that, although live next to people, it is difficult to notice them. You already understand that they are the ones who often spoil our mood, they like to scare both you and your family.

My assistants were happy to explain to you whether you should be afraid of them or how you can tame these monsters, or completely drive them away!

How did it go? Were you able to make friends with them, or at least with a few of them?

Did you really try taming or hunting any?

Then, you are a great fellow! I'm proud of you!

In this, the second book, my friends will introduce you to even more of them, and you will learn how to stop being afraid. We are often scared of what we do not understand or do not know.

You can even find out which of them is which! A great achievement!

Yes, monsters are amazing magical spirits, they are mischievous and fun, well of course, not the Screaming and Grumble Monsters (who are described in other books).

I'll let you into two little secrets that all the monsters of the world share. Monsters fear, more than anything else, that they will suddenly not be noticed by anyone. That will mean, no one will be afraid of them anymore and they consider this even worse than not being noticed!

They are all very cunning, they love to pretend, hide and joke, they cannot be trusted. So, you will have to catch these monsters one by one and not let them do their bad deeds.

I'll tell you how to do it, and the rest is up to you!

So, are you ready to meet the new monsters from this book? I think that some of these monsters you can be friends with, not all of them are bad.

However, think for yourself, it's up to you.

Let's get started!

Gallery of Monsters

The Reflection Monster can be found on many shiny surfaces.

You've may have already noticed but in case you haven't, take a look at your reflection in a christmas tree bauble or a smooth vase. I'm sure it will make you smile!

The reflection will be funny and completely unlike you!

This is the monster's joke on you. It's hard to recognize yourself as the reflection changes your appearance.

It is difficult to get rid of such a monster as it hides only in reflections, but thankfully it is impossible for it to escape from there.

Reflection Monster

Scribble-scrobble Monster

For example, your mother bought you new coloring pencils, a painting set or felt-tip pens and you are sitting, thinking about drawing something interesting and special.

Scribble-scrobble is right there with a plan to take your attention.

Before you realise it, you find strange scrawls and scribbles on the paper. It's the Scribble-scrobble monster whispering in your ear: why do you need to draw, its much easier to scribble lines all over the paper, you won't succeed in drawing something you can recognise anyway!

This is not good advice. Don't listen to him!

Draw the sun or a flower with colourful petals and make your parents or friends happy. Scribble-scrobble will melt away immediately.

It is not only children who are familiar with this monster, some adults are too.

We can all fall under its influence. Have you noticed that sometimes you really want to be capricious, you want to insist on something or perhaps disagree strongly over some trivial matter? Just remember that no one wants to listen to your whims or tantrums, everybody prefers to talk in a calm voice.

This monster only lives a few minutes and then melts away. Here you need to endure those few minutes. You can certainly give free rein to this monster if you choose, but why?

Often, I feel ashamed afterwards. Besides, your parents can get angry too, so it's not worth it.

Monster of Whimsicality

Falling Cups Monster

This is a very famous monster and people of all ages know it. As soon as you put a cup or glass near the edge of a table, that's it, this scoundrel will suddenly make an entrance! Your elbow will undoubtedly knock the cup to the floor.

I'm very familiar with this monster and I no longer put anything on the edge of the table anymore, I keep an eye on it.

How about you?

A word of warning: A defeated Falling Cups monster can turn into a Spilt Drink Monster.

This monster is great friends with the Twilight Monster. As soon as it begins to get dark, the Twilight and Corner monsters giggle, tap, and whisper quietly in the empty shady corners of any room.

You should not be afraid of them; they are absolutely harmless.

Monster of Corners

Attic Monster

This monster is familiar to everyone who has an attic or loft.

At any time of the day, it can create rustles or scratching sounds. At night, you can hear it better and so, everyone thinks that this monster appears only at night, I assure you that this is not true. He really likes the attention of a person at any time.

After his sound, he listens to see if anyone has paid attention to it.

I have wondered many times who it could be there, in the attic, and then I realize that the attic really is empty.

If you knock or scratch the wall back, he will be silent for a long time. I'm very pleased with myself on discovering this!

This monster is considered not good at all.

It's not very good to want something that someone has and you don't. Instead, you can and should approach them and honestly say that you like your girlfriend's hairstyle, or a friend's toy, or a new shirt.

Your friends will be pleased to hear this.

You will then notice that the harmful monster that can easily spoil your mood, vanishes.

Monster of envy

Werewolf Monster

I named him that because this monster knows how to change your mood, that is, your mood can suddenly change for the worse and you don't know why.

Mum asks, "What's wrong?" and you don't know what to say.

My advice is to quickly eat something delicious; even something small like a sweet, a piece of chocolate or a spoon of ice cream.

I assure you; this will quickly cheer you up and this nasty evil monster will no longer be there.

The Sleeve Monster is the funniest monster in this book.

Never get angry if you can't get your arm into the sleeve when you put on a jacket, shirt or blouse.

This is the only trick it has. A one-trick Monster!

As soon as you laugh, the monster will melt away, and everything will work out fine with your clothes.

Sleeve Monster

"Dunno" Monster

This monster is a bit weird.

To any question, he tries to make you answer: "I don't know!"

Being truthful is good and correct! In some cases, it is better to think about your answer.

If you truly don't know, ask more questions to find out what's it about? When being asked about something that is lost, help them find it.

It all depends on the circumstances.

You may not know something, but you can learn and your world will become richer, brighter, kinder and much more interesting.

This Monster lives in puddles. They are as simple as that.

It is always there, as soon as a puddle appears, you know that it already has its special inhabitant.

There it lurks and waits for someone to look into its puddle.

It may not necessarily be a person; it can be a dog or a bird.

It is happy with any creature.

Look into the puddles you find, maybe you will see its laughing eyes.

This monster is absolutely harmless.

Puddle Monster

Rumble Monster

This reckless creature loves noise, any noise, preferably very loud ones.

His favorite time is when there is a thunderstorm close by with roaring thunder.

Since this does not happen often, it is eqully pleased by less dramatic things: drums, a fallen pot or chair, someone shouting for no reason, the knocking of a hammer or the noise of an electric saw, and many more.

If you don't have a drum at home and the pots don't fall, then the monster is probably busy somewhere else in an apartment or house where renovation is underway. This monster loves provoking and is very energetic as he does not sit in one place!

This is a particular example of those Monsters who like to prevent people from concentrating and doing what needs to be done. Lack of Concentration Monsters to give them their full title.

Lacing up shoelaces properly so that they don't come undone is the one I've described here.

I know one adult man that threw away all his laces and replaced them with elastic because of this monster. It had irritated him so much since childhood.

My advice is to start tying your own shoelaces, think about going for a walk, and don't give in to the Shoelace Monster.

One day you'll tie your shoelaces automatically, this monster doesn't like that.

Shoelace Monster

Flower Monster

The Flower Monster is found near flowers, and is friends with the Smell Monster.

Each flower, even the tiniest, has its own aroma.

If you smell a flower and it doesn't seem to smell at all, it's clear right away, what this monster's trick is.

Smile and tell the flower that it is very beautiful. Everyone loves compliments and good words, even a flower.

I think the flower will be able to get rid of the monster then and give you the pleasure of the most delicate aroma.

The Gluttony Monster makes you want to taste and eat much more than is good for you. More than one piece of cake, all of a chocolate bar, several bags of crisps or snacks or even all the biscuits that are left in a packet.

This monster doesn't know about measuring anything. It reminds you in a variety of ways that it's so nice to eat those cookies or apples or chocolates, even when you've just had lunch and aren't hungry at all.

To get rid of the Gluttony Monster, there is a small rule: do not eat anything between these times: breakfast and lunch, lunch and dinner and between dinner and bedtime. Do not take even a tiny morsel in your mouth, it will tempt you to take more.

I tried to get rid of this monster myself and I did succeed, although it was not easy. I think you should try to do it too.

Gluttony Monster

Begging Monster

The Begging Monster loves the word "Give!"

A boy or a girl sees something interesting at a friend's place and immediately the monster is right there: "Give it to me I want a go, buy it for me daddy, I want one of those too!"

This monster does not want to hear about any reasons, does not make concessions, he wants everything in the world, at once, right now.

A very annoying Monster.

You will have to learn how to catch him and rein him in, if you have been acquainted with it before and no longer know each other, then you're a great fellow.

This monster is very hot-tempered, and even rude. He's right there if you don't like something.

It is he who whispers in your ear: "Push or slap the person and the yelling will stop!" You need to fight only as a last resort, it is better to try to negotiate with the offender.

For example, explain what you don't like, and if that doesn't work and the offender's monster is stronger than yours, you can run away, or you can respond to the harmful one.

The monster will tell you.

Brawl Monster

Monster of Boredom

I don't like this monster much but it can be useful sometimes.

It is said that he is very talented and helps people when they are bored.

It helps them develop new and interesting ideas.

You can get bored, but you should not give free rein to this monster.

I got a little bored once and the monster helped me come up with something new and interesting which I enjoyed doing.

A touchy monster often clings like a hook to those who like to be offended by trivial things.

He hangs out and whispers into your ear such phrases as "this is the time to be offended", "be offended, otherwise they will not understand how serious this is", "be offended, maybe they will buy it for you" and so on.

If this monster visits you, immediately remember how many people are happy and love you, remember how many times you were treated and were bought something.

Imagine that this is the time they don't buy it.

If you can skip this moment, you'll see how the monster of resentment breaks up in a couple of seconds.

Resentment Monster

Refusal Monster

Yes, there is such a Monster.

As soon as you hear "I don't want to, I won't", you know that someone is fighting the Refusal Monster.

Yes, you may not want to do something, and you need to talk about it loudly and confidently, but if your refusal grows like mushrooms after the rain: "I don't want to walk, I don't want to eat, I don't want to sleep, I don't want chocolate, I don't want, I don't want it, I don't want to."

It's time to deal with this monster and put it in its place!

Oh, this monster can scare anyone, which he will be very happy about.

He likes to slightly open the doors of cabinets, doors to rooms so that a creaking sound is heard.

This immediately attracts attention, and the monster is happy.

The main thing here is to pull yourself together and understand that most likely it was a draft, and there is nothing to be afraid of!

The monster will realize that it has been exposed and will disappear.

Ajar doors Monster

Our tour of the second Monster Gallery is over.

I hope you enjoyed it!

Be bold, curious, always ask questions, ask out loud, in a firm and confident voice!

Sometimes you can say it to yourself, of course, but its more effective said out loud.

Good luck to you. See you again next time!

Thank you!

Special thanks for the practical advice to Leslie Harwood, an excellent translator and kind editor.

You can find and buy books from our project on the website:

https://thehappystorygarden.co.uk

WELCOME TO THE HAPPY STORY GARDEN

www.ingramcontent.com/pod-product-compliance
Lightning Source LLC
Chambersburg PA
CBHW051319110526
44590CB00031B/4411